ANCHORED

ANCHORED

POEMS

FRED RAGSDALE

With a Foreword by
CARLO COPPOLA

Square Wheels Press || Los Angeles

Ragsdale, Fred, 1972-
Anchored: Poems
ISBN: 979-8-9998555-0-3
Library of Congress Control Number: 2025917580

Disclaimer:
Some of the recipes in this book of poetry include raw eggs. Raw eggs may contain bacteria. You should not feed raw eggs to babies, small children, or pregnant women.

Cover Illustration, pen and paper: Fred Ragsdale

First Edition

Square Wheels Press
5478 Wilshire Blvd, 200
Los Angeles, Ca 90036
www.squarewheelspress.com

In memory of my father,
the gentlest of men;

and for my children,
Marley and Coltrane,
may you know your father.

TABLE OF CONTENTS

Foreword...xi

Preface xxvii

Ornate On the Inside 3

Under A Tree at Lunch 4

My Kitchen in The Dusking... 5

Hiding in A Field of Cotton.. 6

A Thought Before Sleep.. 7

Before She Was My Wife 9

Night Bacon for Three Weeks... 10

Dreams of A Pastoral Winter.. 11

An Anchor System in Decline 13

An Afternoon Swimmer On the Lake as I Stop for Gas 14

A Stenographer 16

At Play 17

To Live Like a Dolphin in A Rainbow Lake 18

Sunset in LA 19

Song for Dead Poets 20

Morning On a Bridge... 21

Woman at A Crosswalk On Cochran Boulevard.................................... 22

Waiting for The Library to Open 24

Another Love Poem 25

Portrait of A Poet 27

Vermont Freshman 28

Children in Utah 29

Nightmare 30

To Wander Alone 31

Morning Beneath the Surface 33

Revolutionaries Lined Up Against a Wall 35

Two Poems from an October Morning 36

The Composition of the Light at Lunchtime 38

It's Just Amazon, Darling 39

Two On A Los Angeles Moon 40

A Trip To The Principal's Office 41

Progress Is Never Simple 43

Blocked. I'm Blocked and Watching Walls and Walking Rooms 44

To A Girl 45

Violence of Lost Gods 47

The Quick and The Slow 48

Pantages Alley 49

On A Rooftop with A Novel as The Sun Has Set 50

The Boy from Wooster, Ohio 52

Chaos in The Double Pendulum 55

My Walking Commute 56

Wednesdays in A Warm Climate 58

Quick Snack with Coco 59

Waiting for The Dawn 60

Engineering A Memory 61

Trying to Kiss a Girl 62

Late Night with A Book 65

Storm Seen from My Office 66

Fatherly Advice 67

Sky High Like a Funny Looking Bird 68

Recordings of A Father for His Children 70

Living In An Octagon 73

Ode to The Charnel Grounds 75

Opening Lines 81

Acknowledgments 85

About the Author 87

FOREWORD

On Being Needled by a Poet

Dr. Fred Ragsdale and I would have likely never met if it were not for my daughter, Johanna. Concerned with my health at my age (old), she informed me that she had checked out a number of LA acupuncturists who make house calls and had determined the one of them I should be seeing: Dr. Fred Ragsdale. The name of his practice —"1000 Folded Cranes"—was compelling, for the crane is a particularly powerful icon, notable for its various literary and cultural connotations in East Asian cultures, among them wisdom, peace, honor, and longevity. It would not be difficult to parse the name of this practice as it relates to what Dr. Fred Ragsdale strives to achieve as a professional.

Checking out his website for the first time, I 'met' not only him but his smiling family as well: Dr. Fred himself, bearded, perhaps in his middle or late thirties, his beautiful wife, and their two beautiful, not-camera-shy children, a daughter and a son. This picture alone, I determined, would make anyone looking for an acupuncturist call for an appointment immediately.

At our first meeting I found him to be congenial, articulate, and vigorously extroverted. My wife, who was rushing off to work when he arrived, met him briefly as well and reported that he was "very good-looking" (or was it "very cute"?) to the family at dinner the next day.

Thus, we began to meet weekly to address the major problem of the persistent pain in my shoulders and lower back. During this time, we talked a lot. A whole lot. I quickly learned that he had travelled widely, living overseas for sixteen years—Europe, Africa, Middle East, East, Southeast, and South Asia, variously—alone, as a "vagabond" (his word), then with his wife, and then for ten years with the children.

In addition, Dr. Fred is remarkably well read. A proud English major from UC Santa Barbara, he spends his day off—Wednesdays--in the Fairfax Branch Library ... reading. Name a novel—he's read it, and very likely several other works by that author. Ditto short-story writers. For example, *The New York Times* had recently featured a spread on the American writer Flannery O'Conner, whose newly discovered paintings were on exhibit at her local college and former residence in Milledgeville GA. I mentioned this to Dr. Fred, for he had earlier indicated that he spent a decade or longer teaching himself how to paint. He immediately brought up one of O'Conner's best-known short stories, "A Good Man Is Hard to Find." In it, an overbearing, rather nasty grandmother and her family are traveling by car to Florida. Their car gets stuck in a ditch, and they are set upon by three escaped dangerous convicts, two of whom kill the grandmother's son, daughter-in-law, and two children. The grandmother is spared, as she tries to convince the leader not to kill her, appealing to the human bond they share as children of God. In her interchange with him, she is transformed into an empathic, understanding, supportive mother figure who touches his shoulder. The leader, deeply rattled by what is, to him, her strange, menacing talk and her touch, shoots her.

The story addresses the divine mystery of God's grace: What is it? Who receives it? And who rejects it? Dr. Fred and I then proceeded to have a rather high-level, extended discussion about grace, even daring to offer answers of a sort to the previous three questions, both of us drawing upon our experiences in classes on theology with the Jesuit fathers, he from high school, me from university. We agreed that while our answers were likely muddled and wrong, and maybe even heretical (we both seemed to relish this possibility), we both admitted that we had very likely received such grace ourselves at various times in our lives, though with not so much as a clue that we had. Moreover, there are people in his poems who have likely received such grace this way as well.

We would have similar weekly discussions on other literary, political, and historical topics where we share similarities in varying degrees; but also food and wine, and, proudly, our kids. Here, Dr. Fred and I have a commonality as well: How we named them. For example, his two children's first names are the last names of Dr. Fred's two ultimate musical deities, Bob Marley and John Coltrane. I mentioned my daughter, Johanna, at the start of this essay, whom I named after my second-most-favorite composer, Johann Sebastian Bach and *not* after my most-favorite composer, Mozart . . . because I could not find the German feminine form of the name "Wolfgang." (Lucky child!) My son was not as lucky, as I burdened him with my name.

In contrast to Dr. Fred's passion for sports and coaching middle- and high-school athletes, my involvement with sports was confined in the main to the *required* Italian-American-family allegiance to Joe DiMaggio and the Yankees (Indians be damned!) or any boxer on Friday-night TV fights with an Italian last name, Primo Carnera, for instance. Otherwise, I was generally indifferent to them, probably because, as a short, underweight, awkward grade- and high-school student, I excelled in none of them. Moreover, I was invariably— and embarrassingly--the last one picked to be on any team in phys-ed classes. Thus, there was little talk about sports. Except once.

When No. 14 seed Oakland University (where I taught for decades) pulled off the biggest upset of the 2024 NCAA Basketball Tournament against No. 3 seed Kentucky--80-76--in a first-round stunning victory to advance to the second round for the first time in program history. Not only did I get a text from the excited Dr. Fred as to what had just happened, and during our next session he animatedly explained to me in detail what a "Big Deal" this was! I felt proud, of course, and was grateful that I could react with a bit of knowledge when my step-son and son-in-law, both avid sports enthusiasts, would be non-plussed with my 'knowledge' of what happened when I would flaunt the correct usage of the word 'seed' in this context for the first time in my life when, as expected, they contacted me to tell me the basketball story. And I got the impression that Dr. Fred was a bit impressed to learn that my former colleague, Oakland University's basketball coach, was a writer not only about sports-related matters, but, as rumor had it, he had written a yet-unpublished novel.

It also turned out, to my amazement and deep respect, that Dr. Fred not only passionately coaches sports and voraciously reads fiction, but he was also a serious reader of poetry. Mostly the British and American pre-Moderns, Moderns, and post-Moderns: Whitman, Eliot, Pound, and Sylvia Plath, of course; and he seemed pleased to have been introduced to one of my favorite poets, Gerard Manley Hopkins, a British Jesuit. He also read the major poets of other languages in translation: the French Symbolists, Italian Modernists, Russian Dissidents; García-Lorca, Rilke, etc. His interest in and understanding of poetry gradually led me to yet a further discovery:

He not only *reads* poetry ... he *writes* it!

He has done so for the past thirty years. As he describes it, "since scribbling on the back of a napkin to try and impress a barista at an all-night coffee shop in West Hollywood dealing with a broken heart." While I was not sure whether it was he or the barista with a broken heart—no matter!--one's own or someone else's broken heart is always a great theme for neophyte poets to start with.

Somewhere between my asking if he would share some of his poetry with me and—as I learned--his desire to have me read some of his poems, we met somewhere there in the middle. Each week he would share one or two poems. As a reader, I was impressed, for it was readily apparent that these were the work of a bonafide poet with an abundance of talent. I base this judgment on my experience not only as a teacher and translator of literature, especially poetry, but also as an editor of three literary journals spread over four-and-a-half decades, during which time I had probably read, I guestimate, several thousand or more submissions of poetry, fiction, reviews, and essays. (About 8% of these actually saw the black of print.)

***

The poetry in this first collection of Dr. Fred's works reveals the poet (or as one is obliged to say in High Literary Criticism lingo, the 'narrator' of the work, who is not necessarily the author of the poem) in various guises: as lover, as husband, as father, as son, as a poet, and, generally, as an acute observer of the Human Condition at various times in many countries and among many peoples. I prefer to use the term "the poet."

"The Poet as Lover"

> Although I don't set out to write "love poems", the "lover" finds herself populating my writing, which makes sense, as this universal archetype presides over all human experiences: familial, religious, cultural, fraternal, and yes, romantic; and so…, the many women in my poems-- They are a composite sketch, immutable totems along the way that serve as narrative vessels for remembering and the returning.
>
> —Fred Ragsdale

This volume contains a generous number of love poems which show the poet as a sincere lover of women. They form a trail for the reader to follow as the poet passes through the various stages of growth in his understanding women, "The search for the life partner," in which endeavor he has roundly succeeded.

In "Trying to Kiss a Girl," he is "full of restless beginnings," uncertain, hanging between "Hope and Hesitation" . . . mesmerized by the scintillance of red-hair / Sweep[ing] her face / While the haughty twist of her lips breathed out cool drafts." Various thoughts cross his mind, almost stream-of-consciencely—"Hope" giving way to "Hesitation"; then "Hesitation" finally giving way to implied Success, in which all three find ". . . in one another the silence we meet at the end." And this end of the poem is an example found in a number of endings of Dr. Fred's poems: Humor, or what the Greeks called this technique of ending a serious topic with an unexpected humorous twist, *bathos*. After all the action of this poem (except for the ending) occurs, we learn in the final two lines where and when it takes place: "Sitting atop a stone bear in the park with a girl I had just met / Beneath an ice-skate moon." Be on the lookout for poems like these (e.g. "Hiding in a Cotton Field," "Night Bacon for Three Weeks", and quite recently, "To Wander Alone.") They take one by surprise with laughter.

By contrast, the poet in "To a Girl" is clearly more experienced, confident, and adept in making love. So is she. He summons her:

> Girl of my song, whisper your song,
> let it blow forth and disturb the frost—
> ...
> And then she was the night
> pure and deep as pitch was the night
> upon which I had hoped to press gently
> splayed fingers, now squeezed lightly
> along her watery ridges like catching melted plastic
> burning in my hand—
> Always too quick for the molding.

Continuing in the similar vein in "Violence of Lost Gods":

> A weepy drunk in neon green cape turns the corner, wildly,
> spilling her treasures beneath a bus stop bench.
> A bored vaquero squatting in the shadows of Hollywood's wanton
> excess
> holds a stop-sign while dreaming of good tequila and a Friday night
> > dance partner.
> A collision, two mismatched molecules . . .
> And he envelops her in the corpuscular thrumming of his loins.
> Dry and percussive,
> while his ravings
> steers her to a schizophrenic frenzy.

By yet another contrast, "Before She Was My Wife" is a love song in which the poet, having been awakened early one morning in Morocco from "a kink" in his neck, is able to sing of "this girl on the bed / wearing sheets made of moonlight—Pearled in an outline / of raven-black hair." Knowing she is the woman he will marry, he is able to hover over her briefly, assured of his choice, and easily returns to an enraptured liminal state, "the thin border / between a hummingbird / and the ghost line."

***

The Poet as Father

The family resulting from the events of the previous poem allows the poet to speak of fatherhood. These poems are, in my view, particularly affective. "At Play," for example:

xvii

I sit in the low hollow of an oak tree
and I closed my eyes
as I counted to ten
backwards
in French
then forward
in Mandarin
while my children hid
and they filled the fern-bush
with the whispered giggles
of butterflies at play.

After reading this poem, which was written while the poet and his family were living in Shanghai in 2011, I felt a profound feeling of *déjà vu*: I had actually *lived* this poem with my young children much like the poet presents the scene here. It was a cool winter evening, 1968, forty-three years earlier, in India. Three languages were used—Spanish, Italian, and Urdu, which the children were quickly learning in an Urdu-medium kindergarten. There were "whispered giggles," not of butterflies but of fireflies.

Another poem which deals with children is "A Thought before Sleep," a meditation upon a parent's concerns about the maturing of the child during adolescence and beyond, when the child goes off to college, joins the military, or some similar event that marks that 'break' through which the child asserts their maturity by leaving home to 'find' themselves. The poet-father is left to observe, think, feel, and maybe even fret:

My son down the hall, too long for his bed
his teenage voice thickening
as are his once boyish knees.
the ones that in the growing years,
when we still gathered tight in play and he listened to my fables,
would ache in the night and cry out for the balm of his father's
hands...

And his daughter:

> Away at school
> her room colder now that the cast iron baseboard heater
> has had its single louver shuttered through the winter.
> I keep her door open and peek my head to catch a midnight hint
> of all the old versions--
> From zygote to this moment,
> in the hope that I can spot one curious detail left behind, something
> moored in the ice since her valediction.

He concludes, with insight into who he is relative to their changes:

> Thus is this life, defined by a finitude
> not always observed directly, but deduced by the gravitational effect
> of a middle-aged man creeping round the queer corners of his home.

***

The Poet as Son

Before discussing "Ode to the Charnel Grounds; aka: *Grief, Part II*," one of the longest and most complex poems in this collection, let's look at the definition of some terms. An ode-- you may recall from middle- or high-school English--is a formal, lyric poem that *praises* or *glorifies* a person, thing, place, or event; "formal" indicates that it is bound by a *seriousness of purpose*; "lyric" means that it expresses the poet's *strong, deep, personal feelings or observations* in *a beautiful, imaginative way*. Odes are often put to music and sung--for example, Bobby Gentry's 1967 Southern gothic hit, "Ode to Billie Joe," and poet Friedrich Schiller's 1785 "Ode to Joy"--with its refrain, "All men shall be brothers"--in Beethoven's Nineth Symphony.

The first section of this poem's five parts takes place high in mountainous Tibet, where the ground is frozen, thus preventing burial of the dead, and little wood for fuel to burn the corpse. Here, the *rogyapa* ("breaker of bones"), a specialized Buddhist ritual practitioner, prepares a corpse for "sky burial" by cutting away the flesh, to be left for birds and animals, from the bones. These are then "splintered into barley paste for the tasting" by celestial sky-dancers who carry the bones to the sky.

Part Two takes place in an East Los Angeles ICU room where an unidentified patient is dying, despite the "waggle of lines, leads, and drains." We are casually told that the attending nurse has lost an earring, an object which links us to Part Three, Varanasi (formerly Benares), India, on the banks of the Ganges River where a cremation has just taken place. A young boy of the low Dom caste helps with the clean-up and finds a gold earring of the deceased, owner of a tea stall who, pridefully, ". . . never once / Touched fingers while taking his coins. . ." which links us to Part III of the poem…

The East Los Angeles ICU again, where ". . . Coins pilfered from a purse hanging from a chair" are needed for vending machine coffee. Here, we meet the poet for the first time, as he reacts to one of the coins he put in for coffee, a nickel, is rejected. Also on this death watch is his young son, in full athletic gear, who came directly to the hospital from the flag-football championship victory with "his trophy to show grandpa" but was now in need of quarters for the vending machine.

A nurse tactfully tries to have the poet sign "Forms clipped to boards" for the dying patient, his father. But the poet acts otherwise: "I crawl into bed with my father and whisper *"Extremum vitae spiritus edere"* (Eat the last breath of life; or less elegantly, Give up the ghost, or, It's OK to die).

In the last stanza of the poem, the poet says of himself:

> I am the breaker of his bones, the eldest son shorn of hair
> chanting psalms of Charon
> to a man across a field as he gives up the ghost.
> I release him with my breath on his lips
> to chase his father as I someday will
> chase him. I tell him I love him. I love him. I love him.
> There is heat on his heart. He is the mind of clear thought.

And Part IV of the ode ends with a mere four words: "The sky dancers descend," and the cycle repeats itself worldwide, endlessly, as the equivalent being(s) in all faiths lead the newly dead to the Hereafter.

***

The Poet's Varied Observations about Poetry

Lying "Under a Tree at Lunch," the poet accepts his gifts of language and feelings cautiously, for he knows that such acceptance may easily create self-doubt and uncertainty. He addresses the sky as an "old friend" who reminds him that, like the sky, he is "growing old, too." As he ruminates about many events of "Love" and "Loss," and in the moment, he seems to wonder whether the gifts of language and feeling are of any worth, ending the poem with an extremely powerful metaphor:

> I look out from these eyes that have seen certain
> events: Love events. Loss events...
> As I run my hands along the scalloped skin of the crocodile
> who hunts my brain,
> I recognize that poetry is a dead-end street.

It seems that this 'recognition' of poetry as "a dead-end street" was, at most, only temporary, and the writer's block that brought forth this 'recognition' was, for the sake of us readers, crushed.

The poem "Woman at Crosswalk on Cochran Boulevard" offers two poetic observations about women's fashion at two different times—contemporary Los Angeles and Elizabethan England. In contemporary Los Angeles, the poet observes a Muslim woman valiantly struggling to keep her black, billowing burqa under control during what was likely a particularly hearty Santa Ana wind burst:

> And then. There. Can you see it on the rise?
> The fine-point-moment before the downsweep,
> where the vulnerable slip protection and
> the expectations that arrive with a stolen glance
> outfox the sobriquet of what has been defined as *good woman*.

She was not entirely successful, for the poet confesses, "for one second. . . / I snuck a glimpse of her sulk." In another place far from Los Angeles, even today, that "stolen glance" could have resulted in her loss of the designation "*good woman*" to that of harlot, hooker, whore or worse, with consequences for both. For the poet, a hundred or more lashes; for her, stoning to death.

The second poem harkens back to "another lifetime," where the poet asked the beloved whether she was his "Elizabethan lover," tempting him with love-apple

> Slices thrust beneath the accordion-tuck
> of your dresses. Squeezed within the musky caverns of
> your armpits, the estradiol exhalation of scented wild
> as you dance
> dance
> dance

This scene reminds me of the almost required dance sequence in various films—at least a half dozen (not to mention plays, operas, and ballets)—about lovers Elizabeth I and Robert Devereux, the Duke of Essex (a cad, who was, among other things, a poet). She runs from the scene and "knowingly drop[s] behind like breadcrumbs / [which] Lead to certain demise." The poet, like Essex, has "Lustily inhaled and greedily devoured" the "Love apples," putting him "on a one-way journey to hell." In a future poem we may receive a depiction of that particular "hell."

By contrast, "Portrait of a Poet" is an honest assessment of how the poet sees himself relative to other poets. It is night. He seems to be stuck somewhere in a poem. The opening line--with the "tongue slippery down" his neck from a lover who seems to crave his attention--suggests an erotic poem. But it isn't.

He plods on and tries to improvise a train-wreck climax, which doesn't work. Then a burial of "dead gods" by "shapes of light beaten flat by a cut of wind"—which he rejects. This leads the poet to the three-line conclusion, with its truthfulness and insightful originality. Here, with the use of parentheses, the poet unravels and reveals the double meaning of "crib"—as a noun, a new-born child's/animal's bed; and as a verb, "to crib," the act of a writer who copies something someone else has written and passes it off as his own. Then in the third line, what High Lit-Crit calls an oxymoron, more colloquially, a contradiction in terms:

> At night
> the poems I (s)crib(ble) are at the least,
> honest lies.

I was really quite dazzled by what the poet has been able to do in these last two lines: An indifferent, casual evaluation of his poetry with "scribble," within which hides the second meaning of "crib," which every serious writer hopes to avoid doing, and then the oxymoron. A masterful triplet of an artistic feat.

***

Poems in this collection brim with many themes, topics, and moods: love, passion, sorrow; joy, empathy, wit; wonder, poignancy, ambiguity; and much more, authored by a unique literary talent demanding to be heard.

We are listening.

When, Dr. Fred, can we expect more?

—Carlo Coppola
Los Angeles, 2025

PREFACE

Dear reader, these poems are meant to be read aloud. Whisper if you must, but do not race through these lines willy-nilly. They were written with a conversation in my head, aloud, while attempting to make sense of my world during both periods of respite and at other times with two feet hard on the road. If you are so inclined to read through these little thoughts of mine, please do so at a snail's pace. Enjoy one or two at a time. Tuck 'em away. Pick them up days later, stretch the binding and again, enjoy a few more. Read. Reflect. Repeat.

ANCHORED

ORNATE ON THE INSIDE

1.

Dry scratch of white on red brick.
Something to carve in chiseled script.
A name perhaps…

2.

I was alive.
No posthumous Buddhist name given
as I crawled from the dream river
with only a minor gash in my head.
The wandering Anglo now a Jizo statue
suffering roots in his garden,
if not, perhaps, his fossilization in amber.

Relaxed to the in and out warbling
of a tiny helicopter circling above
and always out of sight.
Relaxed my stance;
the whistle of a kettle;

3.

the spell now broken.
And the caramel fringed, box-car clouds
laying their interruptions against the flamboyance
of my Los Angeles morning narrative.

UNDER A TREE AT LUNCH

Though you were painted blue long ago, old friend,
your cracks are beginning to show.
Oh Sky! Damnit, I am growing old, too,
yet, still satisfied lazy lying in the same spot beneath the same
butterfly-leaf tree playing the same game of trying
to name your clouds.

I hunted for my father
in the dying journal of his younger brother.
A man who bled poetry day to day in the short
shadows of a certain death.
Here now and alive, I look out from these eyes
that have seen certain events: Love events. Loss events.
These eyes which blink compulsively
and twist into knots this frayed experience.

As I run my hands along the scalloped skin of the crocodile
who hunts my brain,
I recognize that poetry is a dead-end street.

MY KITCHEN IN THE DUSKING

Immersed in an abstract contemplation
I break breath,
ears pricked to the manic hum of kitchen electronics.
      The *chreep chreep* of passing birdplay.
I steady my eyes on the diagonals
of shadow and Sunday light
and the consequent event of three flowers lined smartly.
Vertical slices of vegetation along my windowsill
in need of constant watering
like penguins in a Scottish zoo and sunflowers face the sky.
The down-slant of soft rust
           of indigo
              of lilac
bends the western edge of these Santa Monica Mountains
stretching from copper sundown to the sea.
Extracting myself from this aesthetic
congealed in pyramid streaks and incarnations
and once given legs to leap by a salacious brute force,
I stumble upon the Logos.
In the womb of an instant,
there is time.
If not, there is always the Mother of God.

And a great gale swept upon the surface
while towers of learning crashed down…

HIDING IN A FIELD OF COTTON

There was a time I suckled the pale color of surprise
along with my mother's milk,
my small grey eyes staring into the annihilation.
Now, I simply wait for the flashing
borne by the god of this small sliver of cold white light
that leaks beneath the bedroom door.
Some static-hiss residue from my childhood
Saturday mornings
echoes the beginning of all time,
though for years
clannish and distinctive as my mentors tended to be,
they believed
at first,
it was simply due to pigeons
shitting on our antennas.

A THOUGHT BEFORE SLEEP

I've always found it more comfortable to write in my bed
when the children are asleep
and my wife performs her stretches on the floor.

The house blackened, I've walked my perimeter—
curtains snapped to their drawn-tight edges like amulets worn
as witch-marks against the goat that haunts the beyond.

And the only light visible:
      The intimacy of beam-spread poured down
      from my bedside lampshade.

My son down the hall, too long for his bed,
his teenage voice thickening
as are his once boyish knees.
The ones that in the growing years,
when we still gathered tight in play and he listened to my fables,
would ache in the night and cry out for the balm of his father's hands.
Most nights now I press quietly upon him when I no longer
find sheep to count, careful to muffle
the creaking laughter of my footfall on his bedroom floor,
until hovering like a hungering angel, I breathe in
that which he breathes out and shares with me unknowingly--
The end-catch of his snore within which his boyhood dreams
come alive,
and the slightly milk-sour

trail at the back of this breath.
My beautiful boy.

My daughter
        away at school,
her room colder now that the cast iron baseboard heater
has had its single louver shuttered through the winter.
I keep her door open and peek my head to catch a midnight hint
of all the old versions--
        from zygote to this moment--
in the hope that I can spot one curious detail left behind, something
moored in the ice since her valediction.
Sometimes if my chest takes a jump with the burn and flare,
I dive into her bed and swim rough through the sheets, not worrying
about the complaints from my wife in the morning.

Thus is this life, defined by a finitude
not always observed directly, but deduced by the gravitational effect
of a middle-aged man creeping round the queer corners of his home.

BEFORE SHE WAS MY WIFE

The morning bright in Morocco as the sun bounces off the
mustard and blue geometries tiling the floor, four walls,
        the ceiling,
prompting sleepy-head meditations on the eternal nature
of a personal god…
Or perhaps upon this girl curled on the bed
wearing sheets made of moonlight--
        pearled in an outline
                of raven-black hair.
My cylindrical pillow tossed mid-sleep to the ground,
I've awoken with a kink to my neck and a sarong
stuffed with underwear and sweaters beneath my head.

And now more awake, something soft and quiet
like skin-smell before the amplification of her body heat.

        I am hovering at the thin border
        between a hummingbird
        and the ghost line.

NIGHT BACON FOR THREE WEEKS

Before I lied to my father, calling a lover
from a payphone outside the McDonalds
across Santa Fe Boulevard,
I watched a one-toothed Vietnamese pork packer
smile as he bit the tip from raw sausage links.
Rushed and harried and out of my intellectual depths
as the onslaught of pinch and cut casings sped by,
I begged him to tell me which belonged to the spicy tray…
and which of these links were *original?*
Earlier, on the overnight shift, I had been dumping
shovels-full of chilled pork bits and industrial spices
before being swept in an emergent tide
toward sausage packaging.
The loneliness that had been *Night Bacon*
gave way to the joviality on this assembly line.
Butchery in reverse,
I fibbed and said I saw a cow shot through the head
while watching from the overhang gallery
during my 2am lunchbreak.

Never *ever* believe the conman who cajoles you with
stories of runny yolk finding its way back into a cracked egg.

DREAMS OF A PASTORAL WINTER

Weighted down by pockets stuffed with soul pearls
and stolen bindi cigarettes,
two grey-eyed boys scamper up a yellow maple
and hide amongst the higher branches,
the ones stripped leafless
and left behind beautiful with the death of
all hissing ghosts.

Two boys of legend
glinted in silvery-green iridescence and
skylarking in horseplay beneath the arc of the infinite
as it sweeps across the bent blue indulgence of a winter's dying day--

    'til nudged up against its westering collapse,
    this blister of a sun
    bursts into a riot of purple feathers and wedges,
        widens and it thins.

But zero is a something
and so they breathe a bit lighter,
    these boys who breathe the moonlight,
and riding the backs of grand animated shadows
scuttle all the way down
    sticky in sap & honeydew
to enjoy the gloaming.

To enjoy the bristle-clean scouring
found in this gloaming.

AN ANCHOR SYSTEM IN DECLINE

The hunt for truffles in a forest—
The foraging of our discontent
often ends in plucked trillium
and whistles that bring the rain.
As the Tibetan moon rises young,
so lay the purple of these shed leaves
littered in bunches through which
we slide our shoeless toes.
You lost your left-footed canvas sneaker
somewhere amongst the mosses and duff
because the aglet on your laces
wore away, and so I, forever our anchor,
the wildcat,
quickly sharpen my sprocket teeth
to chain-stop you from disappearing
over the edge
as well.

AN AFTERNOON SWIMMER
ON THE LAKE AS I STOP FOR GAS

But the wrists were enflamed, the joints tightened by screws
dug deep and bent from a lifetime of benediction to Poseidon
while the long-strokes graceful as whispering swans across a lake.
The silent firs stood regnant and proud as pyramids built by pharaohs
and the dockworkers on their lunchbreak
littered the surface with wrappers while counting aloud in Spanish--

Each out-breath taken. Each in-breath borrowed.

Each bit of liquid earth tilled and furrowed until this glimmering
in its parabolic orbit began in some distant reach
arrived without ripple nor rest past our dock,
and for the briefest of moments,
I saw a wind-like silvering
through the mirror shine on that black lake, and then a flutter.
And all was shattered
in the minor measurements of this world collected and hoarded
like stacked cats in a forgotten attic.

And what should burn and flare a red of
drawn blood given up freely from these wrists
could no longer hold still now that only silvery traces
remained in its wake as wavelets slapped against the pilings

while we watchers quiet. Swaying and
rotting beneath an orange summer sun.

A STENOGRAPHER

On the twenty-third breath, I lost hope in the rebirth of a phoenix.
On his twenty-second birthday he bought a second-hand typewriter
to feel the playful resistance of the keys
and sat behind a four-legged desk in the faint and low-cut autumnal daylight.
And it was a wonder.
He wanted to write about jazz though he struggled
with the drop of his left pinky as it struck weakly at this rarest letter.
He was tone-deaf to the screams from her padded room as green
gypsies fucked inexhaustibly in the meaty parts of her marrow.
She lived as a lemming with slow eyes in a jungle of wildcats who pounced
at the slightest provocation.
There was an appetite beneath the way he handled this girl and her green
gypsies and the wildcats and the moon
and every bit of its sheddings.

Did he press a love letter pledge to come again, reborn
as the copper drip of an autumn sun?

Or, was this simply a trick he used when lost
to help him find the earth?

AT PLAY

I sat in the low hollow of an oak tree
and I closed my eyes
as I counted to ten
backwards
in French
then forward
in Mandarin
while my children hid
and they filled the fern-brush
with the whispered giggles
of butterflies at play.

TO LIVE LIKE
A DOLPHIN IN A RAINBOW LAKE

I guess I am lucky that I remain in my bones
and in these bones, in the breath of my bones,
I carry the softest notes of birdsong.
We men long in the day with work in our feet
our arms
our hands,
often forget that by pulling on knotted strings
we liberate the one true thing.
With the rain outside and the scattering of thoughts
inside, the wait. The wait!
The teal-flowered sash in hand.
River to mouth
to life to dance to love to death
to loam to vapor to low clouds to grey sky
to mountain clouds
to raindrop to my upturned face catch a lick
and a copper buckle rawness tickling my tongue--
        The acoustic signature of rain.

h/t Thoreau

SUNSET IN LA

On my walk home
to the east
into the gloam
into the grey,
I came across
a city-deer down from the Hills
shedding its velvet,
scratching rough against the Chinese
Elms that line this Los Angeles boulevard.
Her nose troughed deep in the discarded brassicas
and other foodstuff, not of acorn nor clover.
Her horizontal pupils ran parallel to
the dynamic range of pink
and periwinkle wobbling at my back,
as if to ask--
How do you quantify seeing ghosts
in the side chapel of an upside-down church?

The DJ on my headphones
mired, once again, in heroin hallucinations,
and so, his brother, the mortician,
moonlighting on the six p.m. to midnight shift:
>*The soothing sounds of a castrato*
>*singing the King of Spain to sleep.*

SONG FOR DEAD POETS

A poet once said language never died in Sylvia's mouth.
Oh, how I wish my humpback whale of a lover
from beneath the green sea
would blow bubble nets to entrap and devour
my sounds, too.

Were I a dentist or a more sensitive paramour,
nimble fingers would probe tongue and teeth
deep inside her mouth
down her throat,
tasting and devouring
trapped scuttlebutt from the scraped residue
of inflamed tonsils burning with vocabularies.

A well-diver, ankles tied in sailor-knots
to stakes posted solidly,
bungee cord jumping down her gullet
discovering metaphors,
reprobate promises of earlier lovers,
poems not yet exposed…

then grabbing, yanking, snatching
like a magician pulls a rabbit from his hat.

Before he saws his lover in two.

MORNING ON A BRIDGE

Beneath spread coils of neon pink
sputtering, stalling, flickering
alongside the flat escapade known as
The Dawn, a samurai to no master
cuts water solid with one slice
of his palm.

Impervious to the smell
of brought dreck
blown in from the bay,
there lies a swell to his stretch.
This monarch wing
addicted to the flickering and
the flickering and the flickering.

These patches of memory
circle in and out
between the mark between his eyes
between the fetch of wave across a green sea.

A man wrapped in bilateral ribcages
demanding relentlessly
to a girl beyond the bridge line
that she explain, once again,
those shallow lines around her eyes
that give them such particularity.

WOMAN AT
A CROSSWALK ON COCHRAN BOULEVARD

I.

The wheel-rise of wind caught quick for one second
her black hijab, sweeping it back, fluttering, hovering,
and before the quickening of her left hand tucked it proper,
I snuck a glimpse of her sulk.

This unflung scarf allowed me to peek between
the echo-less chasms of her damping cloth,
the one woven to arrest all mesmerisms
whistled by bunco-boys on the busying streets.

Black fluted drapery to ward off evil intentions
milked from the copulin of her hidden hips
sweeping in each step,
articulating against the dragline of her skirts.
Unable to accommodate the firm press of these hourglass hips.

The soft shadow of a bloom
black against fold, unfold,
the silhouette of a flare.
Billowing cloth all a'tizzy.
The gentle cadence of the wind and its worries
dancing a liturgy,

wave-like,
throughout the swell and the ripple.

And then. There! Can you see it on the rise?
The fine-point-moment before the downsweep,
where the vulnerable slip protection and
the expectations that arrive with a stolen glance
outfox the sobriquet of what has been defined as *good woman.*

II.
In another lifetime, might you have been my
Elizabethan lover?
Apple slices thrust beneath the accordion-tuck
of your dresses. Squeezed within the musky caverns of
your armpits, the estradiol exhalation of scented wild
as you dance

        dance

          dance,

now run from this forbidden temptation
but knowingly drop behind like breadcrumbs
lead to certain demise.
Love apples,
lustily inhaled and greedily devoured.

The poet on a one-way journey to hell.

WAITING FOR THE LIBRARY TO OPEN

He was a beautiful boy
turned golden stallion
bulky for the wintering
and safe beneath a quilt of clouds.
There is a narcissistic melancholy to writing poems,
to staring out at the drip of autumn locust trees.
The flat ache of a wind.
The man in a playground twirl his young daughter.
The curve of art deco bend the soft light of dusk.
The crumbling of concrete below my feet,
hoping that within the yawning hell of Hades,
broad shoulders of the forsaken
hold we stick-figures aloft
for just a few more moments.

ANOTHER LOVE POEM

Apples come and go—
After all, they are the same, save a few details.
Veins and vellus hairs thus line the horizontals
of me and my pomaceous brothers.
A myriad of particularity,
we interact with the infinite crystal universe
and will continue apace
resting only for the echo.

Be jubilant, my dancing toes!
Be swift and create motion and collision
through your hustle
& the thrill of your guile,
which allows you to ford currents in the wind.

Something loose in the wind
jangles like pebbles in a pocket.

Three coins line a doorway
shining arrogantly in the last gleam of sunslip.
A hop of green lightning etches a crescent notch upon her skin,
which she names
Blemish,
but to me has the feel of fresh cut flowers
rolled between fingers slick with rainfall.
She laughs and tells me that I am mistaken.

In the realm of feminine cunning,
she offers the crookedest of grins,
as if to say, *I'll know you again.*

PORTRAIT OF A POET

Sweeten the plot as I shiver from a tongue slippery down my neck.
It's a mystery without a third act, so I might as well improvise
a climax:

The rumble of an exploding train concusses my tympanic membrane
as the poorly constructed weld in the tank gives in to pressures
and thermal expansions
entombing Sunday churchgoers, a chestnut horse, and three oxcarts
in brandy and thickened honey.

In the mirror--Oh! these shivering and febrile mirrors--I always part my hair
with the left hand,
wondering about these shapes of light beaten flat by a cut of the wind
and the covering up of our dead god quick-like and without remorse.

At night
the poems I (s)crib(ble) are at the least,
honest lies.

VERMONT FRESHMAN

Sleepwalking barefoot and avoiding
sharp corners that disappear into poofs of cool dark mist,
I passed a Mayan wandering a hillside in Vermont.
The greenwood was deep and narrow and
she was scratching at dead birds layered thick beneath
the silver crust of cooled lava. Her blade scraped
a hollow sound from their bones and a beetroot-red river tumbled down
into the slow still of things. Clouds assembled like the paving of ice
broken here
now there
by sun-shafts shot through with an approximation of blue
    disturbing the meek brushings of autumn's end.

A prophecy of some sort as dancers in a circle flickered palely
in the sidewash of firelight.
Revel.
    Revel!
        Reveal the rising of tomorrow's lavender sun.
We awake, groggily.

CHILDREN IN UTAH

Learn the trees. Learn the names of the trees,
these little lines of wood run wild,
as I once learned the names of these rascally street-children
who have shaped my heart.
Wake the wise with one delicate poke of your finger. The magi
stumbling like drunk penguins
chasing butterflies in the memory of a circled sun.
Watch as spiral threads of dreamyarns up-thrust
and weave echoes of celestial dust
like the many moons of Saturn
while heroes cycle dead-calm across
a thin layer of mirrored salt flat.

NIGHTMARE

I.

One shouldn't argue with a ghost.

II.

As the tanzanite sky bleeds cantankerous blues,
thick-skinned cannibals roost outside my childhood home
sharpening spears in low timbrous whispers.
I want to run, but a kindly spinster appears in an apron,
the subtle cut of her sideborne eyes promising an adventure
and perhaps, some answers, if I would only stay my fears.
On the bend of a trumpet--
soft, mallet like notes,
cannibals charge through walls enclosing the peach-colored sun-room
and my mother sitting shiva now joins the fight.
Bodies slaughtered and bloodied and Jesus chuckling on my bed alongside
a tribesman gnawing on a drumstick.
My father, the whaleman, whistles in deepwaters,
engraving large-bosomed sirens-of-the-sea on walrus ivory.
His courage buckling like the ill-cracked ribs of a wind-swept umbrella.
The cannibals gone and someone yells—
Who wants cake?
Jokes are made.
Now we too are the scavengers.

TO WANDER ALONE

1.

And she brushed along the soft-side of my skin
with a loose contact--
now to connect
now to spread
now to bathe in the low rheumy sheen
of a sunlight sit fat and low
in the welcoming bosom
of these Hollywood hills.

2.

If beauty is a sympathy
why must I tug at these strings
that twitch with such dissonance?
If beauty is an affinity
a concord
an agreement
a shaking of hands
a tremor of four hands unopposed and
seen through one closed eye, then why

3.

is it the work of inches that frightens me off course
this dream I dream
often

of a grand man? What to do however
in the quiet moments between grandiosities
while the sun settles and fails to blaze.

MORNING BENEATH THE SURFACE

1a.

Aged and alive,
a storm that feeds on
other storms.

    1b.
    The mapping of these ripples moving along the topside
    outward in waves from my love toward one girl
    toward my cyclone fear of one death.
    Now seen from some safe distance.
    Now unseen.
    Now hidden within cracks that
    leak shafts of sunlight
    like dust strike soft at the surface.

    And me drowning beneath all these shadows,
    though never able to remember who it was
    that pushed me under.

2.

Up and over this blue crest of a road
I know now
I trust now
my bones won't break

and the sideways-glance catch the sunshine arise
masks seven palm trees all aligned:
This is the morning in my city.

REVOLUTIONARIES
LINED UP AGAINST A WALL

It is the field of the wild, tangled
in a snarl.
They are after all
weeds and not men
and so limned by each catch of moonlight
beneath the drift of warm rain,
beneath stars that flash and flower,
they slur along this asphalt road--
      that which passes through ghost-towns
        and boom towns alike.
And the incoming wind,
this sorcerer's wind,
whistles as I place my ear to the ground
and I listen for the better lines
that swarm the dawn
and the learning that arrives with a sleep
that is now and forever low.

TWO POEMS FROM AN OCTOBER MORNING

I.

The hum of incoherence
as spun bones creak to wake—
Sleep is for suckers!
My ears strain for the odd dull ring
of a hammer on soft steel.
The tinnient roar
trapped deep to its echoes
as trash trucks trick my ears
and press forward toward the dawn.

Morning arrives, eventually,
in upside down images
that fan outward from my toes
toward a slantwise climb of morning light.
It is as though that which hangs momentarily
and hides in corners within fractal curves
now slices violent through the dawn
igniting sputtered dustmotes
and orbits in reverse,
carrying birdsong in the scattering.

As I write poetry in the dark
I find it far simpler to joke about six rectangles
of lamp-shine
that lazily mimic the moonlight.

II.

There is a quiescence to the color peach
leaked warm through a blanket of fog
when the morning soundings drone deep and distant
and the boulevard shakes to its awakenings.

There is the tree I built tall.
I built well
like a god without the shortcomings.
It reaches line-high into the mists
and I recall with rising amusement
a ball bouncing.
A child laughing.

The purple blooms and the bitter smell of coffee
break my fast and out of the turning
there is a cosmic chittering of morning birdsong
come to me and sing.
I watch as one black-bib sparrow redoubles her efforts
through the thickening of the day.

One becomes six ignites a flare across the pollen-thick sky.

THE COMPOSITION
OF THE LIGHT AT LUNCHTIME

He pieced his thoughts together, this puzzle
that clattered in and out of sequence,
before he brought them to whisper
and then to her ear--
> *I was searching for something foreign*
> *when I tripped into two thousand years of*
> *your laughter.*
Bemused, she answered with a
sour heat on her breath,
irrevocable as a bouquet of wilted flowers
once lay dying within her breast.

And though she stopped short of sharing
the beginnings of her depths
flecked red and still hidden,

this young woman, granted sharp at the edges,
was not without her mischievous and boyish charms.

IT'S JUST AMAZON, DARLING

To adjust yourself to current conditions--
current circumstances
current flow systems--
that give birth to shape and structure
and time
and in a flash produce the architecture,
the good bones that gird this body--
>Always and forever,
>this body.
Choral chants, nevertheless,
reverberating in stereophonic
thump
>*thump*
>>*thump.*
Someone at the door.
Baseball bat in corner.
Fear creeping up my spine with electric titillation.

TWO ON A LOS ANGELES MOON

1.

Beneath the green luciferase moon,

seductive and benevolent

to the shaping of chaos in the stars:

      a gift from the favorite of Plato's lesser gods:

         Jehovah;

      or, as he is known to his closer friends:

         The morning sparrow cross the sky;

      to his beloved:

         The delightful hidden universe;

      and to we vaguely defined sinners:

         He who is found at the beginning…

            but never ever

            shall we meet him at the end.

2.

Shhh… Shhh…

Listen as we float down from the diving-edge

of an angel-white meniscus moon

circling upon this Jungian Orphan squatting on a curb

outside a poorly lit convenience store.

The echoes of his archetypal drift and loss

ring out like the glass shards pulled from his reddened knuckles

and dropped one-by one into a right-side-right

aluminum bowl now lay at his feet.

The aftermath of her hasty exit and a mirror at arms-length.

A TRIP TO THE PRINCIPAL'S OFFICE

We interpret our senses to conform
to child-like expectations--
        A synesthetic tug of texture
        carries the tinnient roar of an echo.

I smell coconut leak from this cardboard box
and soon a sojourner through the deceptive hollow
between truth and some realm of illusion,
call it what you may.

I sit square to my third-grade desk
and the languid pull of schoolboy scissors
dull from tip to heel, slices ragged and untrue.

But oh, find me a compromise!

Sharp to cut clean the pony-tail
hanging in soft sheen
that irritatingly swishes down her neck
and whisks my desk each time
this teacher's pet answers with hubristic delight.

Not knife through butter.
Not blade through soft steel.

Knife through flesh, field dressing a womb that carried
a future star. Now a neutrino. Now zipper-shut closed.

PROGRESS IS NEVER SIMPLE

"Purposive,
or perhaps
accidental; *this life*," sighed an older version of me,
woolen socks coming un-darned one thread at a time.
And yet bits of me remain. A residuum.
There are still certain surfaces I will not scratch
as I lack access to the balm
that stops the spirit from bleeding through my skin.
Instead, I dry-lick the back of envelopes
to quell and contain certain memories
listening for the suncock cast its bellows
across the bronze mornings of our equinox.
All the while, relying on outdated heuristics
as the architecture that girds my flim-flammery
and like pure radium,
allows me to move breezily along
the silvery white snail-trail of my errors.

After all,
we gawk in awe at the bubble jowls of the trumpeter
who blows and blows and blows
as if anything less would mean the end
of his song.

BLOCKED. I'M BLOCKED AND WATCHING WALLS AND WALKING ROOMS

1.

Instead of sleeping when the hour was late,
I walked to my kitchen quiet as a kitten to catch what I could of
the brightest stars in the night fanned out like hurled water in a freeze.
I conspired to write a poem about a lover
once enjoyed in the middle of a June
monsoon; to put flesh on my words.
To put words to her flesh.
But instead found myself thinking on the Hasidism and their hats.
Torus ringed and fur-wrapped with the tail of a grey fox,
the proud inversion of a Napoleonic proclamation
now to be worn as a crown.
The ornamental stuff of the universe
arrayed in sable-like strings of light
linking the believers to the call
and the call to the hoped-for response--
      In the litany between the here and the out-there.
Though to be completely honest,
a bit too Eastern-heavy like Pushkin or Gogol
for our Saturday morning city in this desert.

2.

A word of advice to the muse of a poet:
Never offer them an accolade.

TO A GIRL

Sun-fall in her voice.
She was born of the elements,
born to hide a life in her hands,
born to the drift of a late-afternoon light.
Girl of my song, whisper your song,
let it blow forth and disturb the frost--
a whorling closed-loop vortex all the way through
to the end of it.
But just before
let it be pure suspension.
Let it cleave a self unto two,
perhaps, as a surprise, an un-selving.

And then she was the night.
Pure and deep as pitch was this night
upon which I had hoped to press gently
splayed fingers, now squeezed tightly
along her watery ridges like catching melted plastic
burning in my hand--
always too quick for the molding.

If I once had hopes of setting her to right
by powers vested in me and wholly determined
by my own wants and selfish needs,
then by placing her to dry atop a windowsill,

sunning in the noon-day balm of this city,
surely, disappointment at her scurrying nature
has always brought me back to this present-state
in a room alone and balancing on one foot.

VIOLENCE OF LOST GODS

Wandering in the violence of lost gods,
a weepy drunk in neon green cape turns the corner, wildly,
spilling her treasures beneath a bus stop bench.
A bored vaquero squatting in the shadows of Hollywood's wanton excess
holds a stop-sign while dreaming of good tequila
and a Friday night dance partner.
A collision, two mismatched molecules-- *slam bam, thank you, ma'am,*
and he envelops her in the corpuscular thrumming of his loins,
dry and percussive,
while his ravings
steer her toward a schizophrenic frenzy.

He has forgotten the names and saint days of cousins and earlier lovers,
but this? This is a reckoning.
The simmer before a burning begets a roar. A catechism alive
to spit wild ruinous waste between
lips sweat-tipped and venereal.
It's a rage licking its wounds and awaiting an opportunity to strike,
thrashing against shackles drilled iron deep and once thought secure.

Sparks of his fury scatter like fireflies
ferreting into the coal-soaked blackness.
Portending, perhaps, the arrival of the bulk of it.
The no-longer held back weight behind the tiny embers,
until it can no longer
not devour the wind and the screams of stars long dead.

THE QUICK AND THE SLOW

The quick flow of reindeer
runs the woods
like the slow flow of a thief at night
runs a nightingale floor.
This obscure rigging of a life
scribbled in musical notation
reveals that my thoughts of God,
        these subtle turns beneath the evening lights,
are simply thoughts of Me.
The intimacy of this god is mine.
Mine alone to weave along looms
tangled and looped like the shorn hair of a sinner
        snared in a drain.
I am the call, the echo,
and the response to the immanent,
as only I can see the outcomes,
        caged in flesh am I.
Asking nothing more than before I die to you,
might I strip the excess from these bones
to balance scales I have often considered ungraciously
        misaligned.

PANTAGES ALLEY

At night, in the velvety-patch between the witching and the wakening
beneath a pool of lamplight,
lurk those that savor flesh,
though not by necessity
as when the theater crowd spills into their alley of absence.
At those times,
those magical moments,
the ravishing tends toward a sort of hide-and-seek
played by the demented-ones:
>All pure line and confident curve.
Collecting trophies.
Swallowing dreams whole.

But in this deepening, when even the wind-goddess stills her breath,
there hums an agitation.
An autophagia
gathering in pace;
consuming overworked tendons and sinews
like broken angels devouring the ice-cold miscreants
who flee from their chosen god's warm embrace.

ON A ROOFTOP WITH
A NOVEL AS THE SUN HAS SET
aka: *TURNING AWAY FROM HER EXITING*

I.

I've lost my kite
sliced
as it flashes in quick long dips like jays
across a low autumnal sunning--
      Oh! You celestial flying thing now run the sky,
won't you gather your friends
striped friends
      these zebra-striped friends
and spotted friends.
Let them encircle my sky-flaring kite
      whirling a dervish
entangling taut strings
until… a flash and a tumble.

II.

I stand now above my own lengthening shadow,
eyes turned from the faint line of mercury
that marks the forever far-away…
that marks the entrance to a darkling plain
upon which dance
Hesperides and other earth-bound nymphs.

I stand now beneath the dark madness of our universe,
eyes turned from the reptilian glint of ancient stars ranging
and roaming--
these Serpentinites of the Sky
rifling through the grey-spread
like spilt gems across a promise board
like eggshells tossed within the hard dark,
        once oxidized and yet forever burning cool.

III.
If one were to measure this dynamic entropy,
the starsweep seen would reach
not along an uninterrupted plane of nightening,
but rather
through raises and valleys,
        arriving with stops and starts.

Paradoxes which only hold true at our margins

IV.
though flail at the arrival
of ten fingers that caress my face,
two feet that leave this room
and one broken heart as she once again whispers goodbye.

THE BOY FROM WOOSTER, OHIO

For Carlo

The boy's uncle was the philandering type,
blue eyes and red-haired Italian
come over from the old country and knew
he had arrived when he wore the dead man's suit around town.

She was high-school young, rosy-cheeked and
generationally native to the flatlands--
A debutante to a used-car empire.

The boy brought her around his home
and though she was intrigued by this brown boy
from *The Hill*
and the teenaged tickling of thin black hairs above his full lips,
she slurred instinctively
at the three stoves in his mother's home--
One upstairs for company
two in the basement for the family.

But what did she know of basements so clean they smelled of spices and soap?
What did she know of Sunday morning high mass?
What did she know of stacked crates filled with grapes from the
Finger Lakes and delivered on a Saturday to be hauled downstairs by

a gaggle of cousins and a murder of boys one day become priests,
crow-like in their step-to-it'ness?
What did she know of an uncle who wore a dead man's suit?

An uncle who always ate upstairs
and walked around town in a dead man's suit.

Wore it to church though the dead-man
had celebrated the Sabbath on Fridays.
Wore it because he was lean and built homes
and made a name for himself,
come over from the old country and
slept with other men's wives before the last cry of their liturgies
when they worked double-shifts at the mill
and continued to wear these wives' bodies
warm
long after their men had quit the work of the living
and the bolt ran forever on their world.

His uncle's wife always quiet when the rains came
and ate her meals next door
with her sister, the boy's mother,
in the basement
and who was once introduced to the rosy-cheeked girl
by the boy with a mumbled *Zia,*
which made the girl think of tsetse flies and laugh and laugh
because the boy was so nervous and
couldn't remember ever knowing his aunt's name.

Though years later,
when his uncle was back in Abruzzo with his blue eyes,
building roofs and indulgences for a cousin's cloister
while performing virile feats of strength,
the boy now a man would sit amongst his books
amongst his well-tended standards
and remember catching quiet his aunt once
in the golden sundown of Northeastern Ohio between the houses
leaning against a fence after hanging on the laundry line
a dead man's suit.

CHAOS IN THE DOUBLE PENDULUM

What is the relation between one atto-second
and the age of the universe?
Attaboy, these questions can
and should be asked
while probing folds in my pinky
through the transparency
of a glasswing butterfly.

The sky is ascendent. Moil and swirl.
A reindeer cyclone of cloud and sky disorients,
and for once, I look away.

Fine drawn illustrations of a dynamism: Me,
that is sensitive to the next step—
Deterministic? What if I turn heave-to
and return down the mountain
careful as a cat?

Huge chunks of pinkened whale blubber
pass high over our heads and rain down
like pink confetti. The toss of things.

MY WALKING COMMUTE

I.

I came upon mechanistic secrets
      these engineering delights
            the knobs and the bobs
            the wires and the agitators
as though hand-held through a hushed entry into mysteries
once known only to high-priests showered in chalk-dust
and ivory tower cuckoldry:
      The inside guts
      of a discarded vacuum cleaner
      racoon-ripped and blooming innards
      like dangling ivy hug a highway wall.

II.

Tufts of urban weed littering Olympic Boulevard
spin in the wind. The storm is a'coming!
The storm is a'coming!
Small eddies of paper cups, pinecones, and plastic never-to-bes
swirl beneath the dancing feet of this Child of the West.
A child of the sundown westering,
I rarely wake to the East on its arrival,
but when I do, I fall to knees, to tears,
to recitations of a liturgy that is never shy in its praise
of the sublime
of the cobra coiled day-rise drawing pinks and un-utterables

from beneath a jagged shelf of north-south peaks
like pulled huckleberry sprouts
from the stingiest roots of my springtime thawing.

WEDNESDAYS IN A WARM CLIMATE

They say that deep space smells of seared steak
and within these stars burning cool green
lies the lonely rippling of stones that ring out.
       Successive ripplings are unrung…
            such exaltations
            discovered in our ordinary scraps of life!

A smile here.
            Fingers brushing away split-ends
            that crowd her mascara-hooded eyes,
                   there.

The holding tight of two incontrovertible illusions:
            Horses galloping upon a tomato.
            The sun flaming straight and true.

A pastiche plucked from silent meditations as
I cross these streets toward an oil drum hold a fire
warming ungloved hands
like Miro working scraps
swept from the flood of dust.
And all the while, the hermetic brotherhood stamps their frozen feet
catching dust-motes in the dark.
Conferring meaning from this stuff
                  of the dirt.

QUICK SNACK WITH COCO

Me, a dawdling poet who stares forlornly
at two skies lay before him with green-grey eyes
chewing daintily in constant fear of the incorrect,
while my teenaged son, the philosopher-of-do
(NOT-do-not)
and the hero of our time,
preaches universal self-reliance
with three cucumber chunks jammed in his mouth.

WAITING FOR THE DAWN

The sugary loam of the early liturgical hours
shrouds gloomily this city at sleep.
Inner circles speak of myths
stacked ring to ring like nighttime promises
constellate the night-sky
while taking no measure of their inevitable debt and penury.

Lemons lie outside shadowed ladders.

Oh! When will you arrive, crack of color?

Green halogen spray catches backlots
empty now that the dancing has quieted.
The early-edition paperboy rests upon stacked bales
humming hymns to the daybreak fire burning
straight through his bones.

Cowled in throw-blankets and carrying a carrot
as an icon, a monk of No-God shuffles through
his lightly lit kitchen counting seconds off his life.

And above all sails the morning sparrow
let loose by the boy
now sleeps softly in the mud.

ENGINEERING A MEMORY

I once read a book in a storm
alongside a girl
and though I had hoped
we'd both sail loosely
along the posture all bodies assume,
it was not until
these years later,
the leaping point
revealed
that we two-twiddled bolts
far from having shared a parallel determinism
had existed solely as intermeshed helical grooves
forever spun around and around and around,
yet never finding any co-existence.

TRYING TO KISS A GIRL

The audible gasp before the convulsion,
before the end,
when the world as far as we could see
was splashed in a shade of Prussian blue
and we lived in the certainty, that if not
for our better angels, a reckoning
cloaked as lightning-quick slips of shame
might just challenge the ease at which we tottered along this slackwire.
A balancing
forever spanning two smooth-faced citadels,
often in communion, though this night wrought in violent opposition:
      Hope

          and

              Hesitation.

Ah, the pathos of a young man
landing with such sublimity,
it simply bursts your heart!

In this, my wonder, and so,
as night deepened into the darker night still,
I sat mesmerized by the scintillance of red-hair
sweep her face,
while the haughty twist of her lips breathed out cool drafts
through the narrow burden of our lives.
I worked hard at my loafing, this studied non-intrusiveness,

so, when she turned her face to the brilliance of the stars,
I, full of restless beginnings,
searched the sky, my knuckles, the swerve of her neck
for some point, some respite
upon which the next moment's defining curve would intersect unto itself
and burst forth a diverging branch of potentials--
            alive and crackling with the elegance
            of the somewhere-out-there.

I struck upon the abstract idea of consulting my *better angels* and
to give it life
amongst her keening laughter--
                this grand amusement--
traced a transversal across some specter
hidden in the air that sat warm and balmy between we two.
I cut deep and sharp and clean
hoping within to discover a man of revelation and subsequently,
discover an even braver man:
            As was once the province of seers in some or another heroic poem.
Though, as they are wont to do,
these revelations slipped thick through my fingers
and into the dust of all things that fall beneath what the eyes can hold
and the heart feels no more.
            Alas, what it feels no less.

In this grasping and in the losing,
I realized the reckoning upon which I depended
had always been written in the two hands, ten fingers,
and nails presently scuffed from many cowardly attempts
at scratching my name unto her wall.

And there as always, alongside the guessing,
decisions
        decisions.
                decisions.

Finding in one another, the silence we meet at the end.

And in this silence that need never explain,
        though not for fear of the questioning,
the quickfallen darkening settled around me
sitting atop a stone bear in the park
with a girl I had just met.
Trembling beneath an ice skate moon.

LATE NIGHT WITH A BOOK

65

Two green moon monkeys dance before a murder
and now, a ghost.
Rooted to the womb of the earth,
he haunts unsuccessfully
quietly slithering between the well-worn intellectuals
who wait out the storm in a library reading room.
These worn-down men! Threadbare and scrofulous
like our train-side sun
rise ripened over the river, polluted and grime-streaked
in purple dyes. Eerily electric in its velvety texture.
Don't they notice the grimace
of the consumptive? Perhaps if I had legs,
I could stomp three times and wake them from
their slumber.

STORM SEEN FROM MY OFFICE

Rain fell in clopping heaps
like leaflets tossed down from some unseen
peace-seeking dirigible
announcing: Lay down your arms!
Arms that link these scurrying creatures
to hands that cling tight their umbrella crook-handles.
On Venus, it snows metal and rains sulfuric acid.
These three kittens sit quiet on a windowsill.
What news do they bring me?

FATHERLY ADVICE

Burning eaves and flying dragons,

eyes glinting sunfire,

populate the fairytales I've sung my daughter

soon traveling to Denmark

and I worry on the Vikings of this low country.

A tribe who gave us dreams

but see no color--

And so the African was *blue;*

and the snow was *blood;*

and the sunrise was *grey*

      leached from stones.

And like the ancient Greeks…

made love to women the color of *wine.*

SKY HIGH LIKE A FUNNY LOOKING BIRD

Dubious of personal experience
and bored with personification,
I write a poem about replication.
A narrative of a gene that instantiates
in the mouth of a poet
in the whispered nothingness of a poet
in the stereo-cilia hairs of a lover of this poet,
steady to his promises…

Such is the gimcrack covering of this world.
Aldous thought it plastic, adorned in man-made
right angles and *pardonez-moi* civilities.
A stroll across the bridge between sand-castles
on which we lay our hopes,
our soul-feedings,
and that which stands anchored to shores wind-riven,
thus, unsustainable.

Though I carry my fears heavy like a snail shell,
I am not a snail! I am not victim to parochial limitations!
I cross from these desert shores to snow-topped mountains peaks
with nothing more than my guile and a fresh toothbrush.

And I am man.
Yet, never able to slip my vertebrate skin
and two eyes composed primarily of water.

Like songbirds ascending to the heavens,
first, we are blinded in the lower celestials
and higher still, these glaucous eyes
are boiled blind inside our heads.

RECORDINGS OF
A FATHER FOR HIS CHILDREN

I.

The elms:
crippled in their autumning
goldenrod in their stitching
deckled in their crunchy-crinkle dusting of leaves
along the sidewalk
upon which I walk
nightly.
But for now,
these sentinels
tunnel me toward
a nowhere.
And an unbecoming.
A place without clocks.

II.

The flippening occurs
eyes closed
maneuvering my car
through the city streets
I've eternally mapped
feeling no need
to rest rheumy-rimmed eyes upon
the blue dot in the darkness

and the barking distances of
obstacles
along the path.

III.
The open road--
        these unwavering delights,
belongs to my children
moving in a deliberate direction outward &
beneath the downpour of bluer skies.
Their endless leave-takings
borne poorly by he that calls upon
some minor deity for relief
while scuddering in herks and jerks
        like a drunkard through this city.

IV.
Here sits the maker who molded this melancholy!
The walker of awkward lines.
He who turns
and returns
pulls on a thread
rends a hole
pokes
he pries
he pulls apart
        exposing the flood.

His valiant effort
to catch the moment
soon taken to its wing.

V.

Beneath banana leaves
strung loose in a longing
gesticulating like a madman.
Playing dance and tumble
cupping watery sunlight
on an island--
live laugh love…

Now trapped in traffic
graying.
The day
settles
grayly.
The hole closes tightly.
The memory now gone.

VI.

In the bloom of stars
flare across the sky,
lives a story…

LIVING IN AN OCTAGON

In memory of Kristin Kulage, 1975-2025

This was an artist's home.
The well-lit nook
where he watched the sparrows
and battled the gods.
Fireplace in the bedroom,
though we once left the flume shut
smoking out our Thanksgiving dinner guests
and later made love in the ash on the floor
like trapped geese in a squall.

I liked to sit firm on my puritan chair and with a flick
of my wrist pull the chain to the pink desk lamp
that you surprised me for my birthday when even my mother,
long in her drink, had forgotten.

I pretended well that I was writing a book on jazz.
I even went as far as to visit the library stacks
covering the long oak table with copious notes
and primary sources before stopping by the liquor store
after you had left me for the lawyer.

Always two bottles of the cheapest champagne.
I had no income nor companion

save two loyal dogs and a small tv on which I watched
NYPD Blue re-runs.

Some nights, I spiraled down the iron wrought stairs
into my garage studio and threw
house paint gone rubbery on stolen canvases.
And though I was a failure in my one-shot exhibit,
often drunk and angry amongst drippings and splatters,
I still believed in art!

       What I learned from a year in the woods
       was no different than any Russian nanny
       portending all inevitabilities
       in the wings of bees.

For I too, watched saliently
the slow-motion shock of the Autumn moon
as it filtered through a rat-crack in the wall
accosting my brush, my wrist, and eventually
every inch of me with a shadow and light interplay
that I would never display
in paint nor poem.

Come the springtime, alone, I laid our picnic rug
within the measured square of a kitchen yard
now vanished of all wall and jointing.
I lunched amongst wildflowers plum-purple
and textured and still to this day
battle-beatened against a poet's stubborn memory,
remain unnamed.

ODE TO THE CHARNEL GROUNDS

I.

While the sky-dancers,
fattened and celestial,
defecate upon the face of this
holiest of mountains,
the *Rogyapa* sleeps among the sprawl
of knives and hammers and
alms for the dawn.

This hieroglyph scrawl
of a man now awakened,
stooped and at work
beneath the ellipsoid of a
westering moon,
  profound in its silvering
  along its edges.

He works the walnut handle on his flaying-
knife with quick and low thrusts,
a gift from a lama
who cycled into dissolution
with a giggle, and now stretched taut
from tent-line to limbs,
thin skin of his achilles tendon scraped clean.
Bones splintered into barley paste for the tasting.

In the faint grunt of broadstrokes that cast no shadow,
this Breaker of Bones dwells not on the *dakini,*
winged angels fed flesh from the Buddha
          to save the life of one pigeon;
nor on the low swarming black mass
coaxed to feast on those less holy than they are common
          by ritual dance and juniper incense.
Rather, he swipes the oil-sheen of sweat from
his tawny brow and smiles down-mountain at the cross-profile
of a river and dreams of his own bones in the sky--
          bones in the sky…

II.
…bones softening beneath a waggle of lines, leads, and drains
crisscross a body lashed to its own Dharma,
its own coarse dissolution among the hushed chaos
of an East Los Angeles ICU where the attending nurse
          has lost
                    an earring…

III.
…an earring flashes like salamanders
skinny between cracks of the paan-stained
pavers leading mourners down to *the* river.

A quick of nimbus gold in the shallow ash
catches this kohl-eyed
Child of the Dom as he darts between
roughly hacked mango wood
          cross-stack
sandalwood

cross-stack

two tulsi sticks

eight feet high and bracing temple walls

architected for this City of Death

epochs upon

              yurgas upon

                          divine years

before Christian gods walked on water.

This young *Untouchable*

deadened to the keening lament of all left-behinds

will never bathe his father in sacred ash and butter-oil.

He will never march his father's shrouded body down sacred alleyways:

Ram naam satya hai.

       Ram naam satya hai.

But on these charred pits of the Manikarnika Ghat,

he holds splendid this found treasure.

Master of the ascendent lightning,

he is the oil and he is the wick

that set these charnel flames a'fire.

All the while his father, this breaker of bones,

whacks viciously at the burnt skull

of the neighborhood tea-wallah who never once

deigned touch fingers while taking his coins…

III.

…coins pilfered from a purse hanging from a chair.

Six quarters for a vending machine coffee,

one rejected, so I eye it to the solar-noon

winking like thin strips of foil

through the poly-carbonate glaze window
and notice it is a nickel. A nickeling of memories
like the wad and cram of vanishing points into a
parachute pack slung over a shoulder to be carried home
and soon forgotten. I scream a death-wail into my fist.

My son, knees muddied from championship flag-football,
cleated shoes slipping and scrabbling to catch purchase
across the hospital linoleum floor, skids to a stop
to ask for more quarters.
He brought his trophy to show grandpa,
old-school ornery with a gentle condescension
toward participation awards,
but would surely celebrate ten-year old victors
and their plunder.

He is a gathering brought us into bloom and now the prayer
to return to ground. To sacred dust. A nurse whispers;
forms clipped to boards.
Vultures wheeling above with the more patient hawks
higher still. I crawl into bed with my father and whisper:
          Extremum vitae spiritum edere.
Now begins the dissolution of the winds.
I am the breaker of his bones; the eldest son shorn of hair
chanting psalms of Charon
to a man cross a field as he gives up the ghost.
I release him with my breath on his lips
to chase his father as I someday will
chase him. I tell him I love him. I love him. I love him.
There is heat on his heart. He is the mind of clear light.

IV.

The sky dancers descend.

OPENING LINES

A poet once said language never died in Sylvia's mouth   20

Aged and alive   33

And she brushed along the soft-side of my skin   31

Apples come and go   25

At night in the velvety patch   49

Before I lied to my father, calling a lover   10

Beneath spread coils of neon pink   21

Beneath the green luciferase moon   40

Burning eaves and flying dragons   67

But the wrists were enflamed   14

Dry scratch of white on red brick   3

Dubious of personal experience   68

He pieced his thoughts together, this puzzle   38

He was a beautiful boy   24

I came upon mechanistic secrets   56

I guess I am lucky that I remain in my bones   18

I once read a book in a storm   61

I sat in the low hollow of an oak tree   17

Immersed in an abstract contemplation   5

Instead of sleeping when the hour was late   44

It is the field of the wild, tangled 35

I've always found it more comfortable to write in my bed 7

I've lost my kite 50

Learn the trees. Learn the names of the trees 29

Me, a dawdling poet who stares forlornly 59

On my walk home 19

On the twenty-third breath 16

One shouldn't argue with a ghost 30

"Purposive… 43

Rain fell in clopping heaps 66

Sleepwalking barefoot and avoiding 28

Sun-fall in her voice 45

Sweeten the plot as I shiver 27

The audible gasp before the convulsion 62

The boy's uncle was the philandering type 52

The elms 70

The hum of incoherence 36

The hunt for truffles in a forest 13

The morning bright in Morocco 9

The quick flow of reindeer 48

The sugary loam of the early liturgical hours 60

The wheel-rise of wind 22

There was a time I suckled the pale color of surprise 6

They say that deep space smells of seared steak 58

This was an artist's home   73

Though you were painted blue long ago   4

To adjust yourself to current conditions   39

Two green moon monkeys dance before a murder   65

Wandering in the violence of lost gods   47

We interpret our senses to conform   41

Weighted down by pockets stuffed with soul pearls   11

What is the relation between one atto-second   55

While the sky-dancers   75

ACKNOWLEDGMENTS

All thanks and appreciation, Dr. Carlo Coppola—poet, teacher, and friend--for his genre-bending discussions, his mentoring, and for being my most supportive reader. You, sir, are a mensch.

My mom. My brothers, Danny and David.

My friends—to those of you who have read my work over the years and to those who are surprised and maybe even confused by the tiny pieces of you that populate my poetry.

And most importantly, my best friend and the love of my life, Lulu. My muse.

ABOUT THE AUTHOR

Fred Ragsdale is poet and a dad, a wanderer and a lover of movies, books, jazz, and baseball. He lives in Los Angeles, California with his wife and two kids. This is his first published volume of poetry. Many more are coming down the pipe.

9 798999 855503